# The EMANCIPATION PROCLAMATION

*"When you are dead and in Heaven, in a thousand years that action of yours will make the Angels sing your praises."*

*—Hannah Johnson, mother of a black Northern soldier, in a letter to President Abraham Lincoln about the Emancipation Proclamation, July 31, 1863*

By the President of the United States of America:

A Proclamation.

Whereas, on the twenty-second day of September, in the year of our Lord one thousand eight hundred and sixty-two, a proclamation was issued by the President of the United States, containing, among other things, the following, to wit:

"That on the first day of January, in the
"year of our Lord one thousand eight hundred
"and sixty-three, all persons held as slaves within
"any State or designated part of a State, the people
"whereof shall then be in rebellion against the
"United States, shall be then, thenceforward, and
"forever free; and the Executive Government of the
"United States, including the military and naval
"authority thereof, will recognize and maintain
"the freedom of such persons, and will do no act
"or acts to repress such persons, or any of them,
"in any efforts they may make for their actual
"freedom.

documents of
**DEMOCRACY**

# *The* EMANCIPATION PROCLAMATION

### by stephen krensky

MARSHALL CAVENDISH BENCHMARK
NEW YORK

With thanks to Catherine McGlone,
a lawyer with a special interest in constitutional law and American history,
for her legal eagle eye in perusing the manuscript.

Other Marshall Cavendish Offices:

Marshall Cavendish International (Asia) Private Limited, 1 New Industrial Road, Singapore 536196 Marshall Cavendish International (Thailand) Co Ltd. 253 Asoke, 12th Flr, Sukhumvit 21 Road, Klongtoey Nua, Wattana, Bangkok 10110, Thailand • Marshall Cavendish (Malaysia) Sdn Bhd, Times Subang, Lot 46, Subang Hi-Tech Industrial Park, Batu Tiga, 40000 Shah Alam, Selangor Darul Ehsan, Malaysia

Marshall Cavendish is a trademark of Times Publishing Limited
All websites were available and accurate when this book was sent to press.

LIBRARY OF CONGRESS CATALOGING-IN-PUBLICATION DATA
Krensky, Stephen. The Emancipaton Proclamation / Stephen Krensky. p. cm. — (Documents of democracy) Includes bibliographical references and index. Summary: "An analysis of the Emancipation Proclamation, with information on how it was created and its impact on American history"—Provided by publisher. ISBN 978-0-7614-4915-7 (print) — ISBN 978-1-60870-671-6 (ebook) 1. United States. President (1861-1865 : Lincoln). Emancipation Proclamation—Juvenile literature. 2. Slaves—Emancipation—United States—Juvenile literature. 3. Lincoln, Abraham, 1809-1865—Juvenile literature. 4. United States—Politics and government—1861-1865—Juvenile literature. I. Title. E453.K74 2012 973.7'14—dc22 2011000182

Editor: Joyce Stanton     Art Director: Anahid Hamparian
Publisher: Michelle Bisson     Series Designer: Michael Nelson

Photo research by Debbie Needleman. The photographs in this book with permission and through courtesy of: Front cover: Thirty five star flag, c. 1862 – 1865. Courtesy of the Cape May County Historical and Genealogical Society, New Jersey. Photo by Paul Pierlott. Portrait of President Abraham Lincoln by George P. Healy, c. 1880. Photo by Katherine Young/Getty Images; Half title page: Library of Congress Prints and Photographs Division. Washington, D.C. (LC-DIG-ppmsca-19241); Shutterstock: ii – v; The Granger Collection, NYC – All rights reserved: 6, 20, 27, 32, 51; © Bridgeman-Giraudon/Art Resource, NY: 8; Portrait of Sir John Hawkins (1532-95) from "Memoirs of the Court of Queen Elizabeth" after a triple portrait by Custodis (d. 1598) published in 1825 (w/c and gouache on paper). Essex, Sarah Countess of (d.1838)/Private Collection/The Stapleton Collection/ The Bridgeman Art Library: 11; © North Wind Picture Archives/Alamy: 13; Male Cotton Picker (oil on panel). Walker, William Aiken (1838-1921)/The Historic New Orleans Collection/The Monroe-Green Collection/The Bridgeman Art Library: 18; © The Art Archive/Jerry Pinkney/NGS Image Collection: 25; © The Art Archive/ Culver Pictures: 31; The Kneeling Slave (oil on canvas). The Bridgeman Art Library/Getty Images: 34; Library of Congress Prints and Photographs Division. Washington, D.C. (LC-DIG-pga-03298): 37; © Lebrecht Music and Arts Photo Library/Alamy: page 38; © Mathew Brady/MPI/Getty Images: 42; Library of Congress Prints and Photographs Division. Washington, D.C. (LC-DIG-highsm-09902): 45; Library of Congress Prints and Photographs Division. Washington, D.C. (LC—USZ62-2276): 47; World History Archive/Newscom: 52; Library of Congress Prints and Photographs Division. Washington, D.C. (LC-USW3-037939-E): 57; © Cornell Capa/Time & Life Pictures/Getty Images: 59; AP File Photo: 61; © David J. & Janice L. Frent Collection/ CORBIS: 62.

Printed in Malaysia (T)
135642

Half-title page: President Abraham Lincoln
Title page: The opening words of the Emancipation Proclamation

# Contents

# A Sign of Things _to_ Come

On the evening of June 16, 1858, a tall, gangly man stood up to give a speech. The setting was Springfield, Illinois, where the man lived and worked as a lawyer. The occasion was his acceptance of the Republican Party's nomination for the United States Senate.

Forty-nine-year-old Abraham Lincoln had thought long and hard about what to say at this moment. Recent events, coupled with decades of controversy over the issue of slavery, had gravely endangered the nation. Lincoln had worked on his speech for weeks, writing out bits and pieces on scraps of paper and keeping them in his tall hat. He had gone over the words repeatedly, making changes where necessary, and finally memorizing the whole thing.

_Above:_ When he accepted the nomination to be Illinois' Republican Party candidate to the U.S. Senate in 1858, Abraham Lincoln gave a rousing speech that included the now-famous phrase, "A house divided against itself cannot stand."

Lincoln's first words referred to the uncertainty of the times, and the difficulty of knowing how best to go forward. He then made his position clear.

"A house divided against itself cannot stand," he declared.

I believe this government cannot endure, permanently, half slave and half free. I do not expect the Union to be dissolved—I do not expect the house to fall—but I do expect it will cease to be divided. It will become all one thing or all the other. Either the opponents of slavery will arrest the further spread of it, and place it where the public mind shall rest in the belief that it is in the course of ultimate extinction; or its advocates will push it forward, till it shall become alike lawful in all the States, old as well as new—North as well as South.

There was more, but the point had been made. For his supporters, it was a rallying cry for freedom. For his enemies, it was further proof of Lincoln's abolitionist leanings. He was a dangerous man and would bear close watching.

Despite an effective campaign, Lincoln lost the election. Two years later, he ran for office again. This time, the stakes were even higher. Abraham Lincoln now hoped to become president of the United States.

Christopher Columbus is known for his discovery of the so-called New World, but he is less known for enslaving the native peoples of the islands he discovered.

# Chapter One

# Slavery *in* America

IF THERE WAS A MOMENT WHEN THE European discovery of the New World did not involve slavery, that moment quickly passed. No sooner had Christopher Columbus, in 1492, set foot on an island he named San Salvador, than he was rounding up some natives to do his bidding.

The natives resisted, but Columbus and his sailors were prepared for that. They possessed superior weapons and armor, which enabled them to impose their will on the local population.

Columbus and the Spanish conquistadores who followed were not the first to employ slavery in the Western Hemisphere. The great native civilizations of North and South America—the Maya, the Incas, and the Aztecs—had their own slave traditions. These traditions, however, were not racially based. They did not single out a specific group of people for servitude. Adults might become slaves in retribution for committing a crime or after being captured in battle. Children could be sold into slavery by their parents.

For the Spanish, the native populations were a means to an end: the acquisition of new lands and the riches they contained. The fact that the lands were inhabited did not trouble the newcomers. Native Americans seemed too different from the Spanish to be taken seriously, or treated as equals. They would, however, make a handy workforce, especially since they could be forced to work for nothing.

## IN NEW ENGLAND

Things were a bit different in the English colonies that grew up in the 1600s on the northeast coast. Unlike the Spanish conquistadores, the first English settlers had neither the strength nor the ambition to impose their will on the local population. Only later, after the newcomers had become more strongly entrenched, would they be willing and able to expand their influence by whatever means necessary.

In the course of not too many years, native populations in the Americas were decimated. The people were exhausted and made ill by overwork and unfamiliar diseases such as smallpox, which had been brought to the continent by the Europeans. The Indians did not make satisfactory slaves for long.

## THE SLAVE TRADE

Meanwhile, it turned out to be more practical to import stronger, hardier slaves from abroad. The first English slaver was John Hawkins, who began his raids along the African coast in 1560. Queen Elizabeth I disapproved of the trade—until she found out how profitable it was. And then, with a powerful Spain always threatening to invade her island, she stopped protesting. Defending England was expensive, and her share of the slave bounty was too lucrative to resist.

John Hawkins was the first English "slaver," or person who imported slaves.

The first Africans arrived in Jamestown, Virginia, in 1619 to work the tobacco plantations. In a few short years—Jamestown had been founded in 1607—tobacco had become a lucrative cash crop. The Virginia planters used both black African slaves and English indentured servants to work the plantations. They soon realized, however, that it was more profitable to have permanent slaves than to rely on the temporary labor of white indentured servants. (Indentured servants worked for a period of time, often seven years, in return for free transportation to the colony. At the end of their contract, they were granted their freedom.)

Over time, the Virginians passed legislation to ensure the establishment of a permanent, unpaid workforce. In the 1660s, the House of Burgesses, Virginia's colonial legislature, passed a law stating that black "servants" and their children would henceforth be considered slaves for their entire lives.

In the meantime, a lucrative commercial enterprise had developed back and forth across the Atlantic. Ships from New England would arrive in West Africa with barrels of rum or other goods, which they would trade for natives captured in advance by their agents. These captives would then be transported to the Caribbean, where the ones who had survived the crossing were sold or exchanged for sugarcane. The sugarcane was then carried to New England, where it was made into rum. At each step of the journey, handsome profits were made. Everyone, except for the enslaved Africans, of course, seemed happy with the arrangement—or at least they were willing to look the other way in return for such financial success. The key aspect of this trading was its efficiency. The ships were never empty, and each leg of the trip brought a sizeable profit.

At first, the captives aboard the ships were treated somewhat decently, not because of good intentions, but simply in the practical hope that they would survive the long voyage. They were not packed in too tightly but were given sufficient room to breathe. After

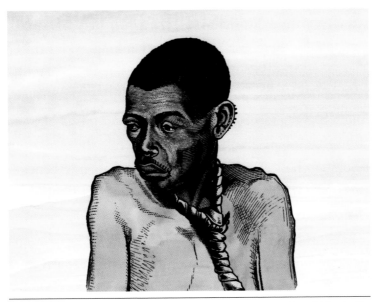

Enormous profits were made in the transportation of slaves from Africa to the Americas—everyone was happy but the once-free people taken as slaves, like this man from the Congo.

a while, though, with a view to increasing profits, the slavers decided to pack in the people as tightly as possible, risking the loss of some in the hope that most would survive—or at least more than if a smaller number were treated better from the start. As this idea took hold, the prisoners were packed belowdecks with just a few inches of space between them. They were only brought up on deck, in chains, to exercise. Some quickly decided that death was preferable to the conditions under which they were suffering. But those who refused to eat were force-fed with a funnel-like device. To prevent anyone on deck from trying to jump overboard, nets were rigged along the sides of the ships and sailors maintained a constant watch.

Initially, there was no concerted attempt to introduce slavery to the colonies. No mastermind was operating behind the scenes, pulling strings to promote its development. Slavery turned out to be useful and profitable, and so it grew as an industry. However, while the American colonists chose slavery because of its economic benefits, the one factor that was to determine who could be enslaved was skin color.

As the 1700s began, black slavery was legal throughout the thirteen colonies. By then, there were 20,000 slaves, and the system of laws they lived under, known as chattel slavery, was totally restrictive. Under this system, a slave was actually owned by the slaveholder, just like a farm animal or a piece of furniture. Chattel slaves were slaves for life, and so were their children. Unlike slaves in other places in the world, slaves in America could not marry. They could not own property. White owners could mistreat them with impunity. Like animals, they might be branded, whipped, and chained. Their owners could even mutilate or kill them.

During the course of the eighteenth century, the slave population in the colonies continued to grow. By 1776, there were 500,000 slaves among a white population of 2.5 million. (In a few Southern colonies, the slave population equaled or outnumbered the white population.) There were some people who protested.

The Quakers, a religious sect centered in Pennsylvania, were among those who publicly objected to slavery. But objecting to slavery and actively doing something about it were not the same thing. An early draft of the Declaration of Independence included words condemning the African slave trade, claiming that King George III had:

> waged cruel war against human nature itself, violating its most sacred rights of life & liberty in the persons of a distant people who never offended him, captivating & carrying them into slavery in another hemisphere, or to incur miserable death in their transportation thither. This piratical warfare, the opprobrium of *infidel* powers, is the warfare of the *Christian* king of Great Britain. He has prostituted his negative for suppressing every legislative Attempt to prohibit or to restrain this execrable commerce, determining to keep open a market where MEN should be bought & sold.

*"He has prostituted his negative for suppressing every legislative Attempt to prohibit or to restrain this execrable commerce, determining to keep open a market where MEN should be bought & sold."*

*—Thomas Jefferson, writing about King George III, in a draft of the Declaration of Independence.*

*The statement was subsequently deleted.*

These words were written by the young Thomas Jefferson, a slave owner himself. The clause, however, could not gain congressional approval. Too many Southern colonies depended on slavery to support their economies. Criticizing slavery was much easier in the Northern colonies, where the institution had little current impact. Still, Northerners were not inclined to criticize slavery too loudly. It was no secret that many of their grandparents and great-grandparents had made their fortunes in the slave trade years before.

The colonists went on to win their independence from England without having to deal with the problem of slavery. However, when the Founding Fathers gathered to draft the Constitution in 1787, the issue came up again. Although there was widespread support for uniting as a single country, delegates from the Southern states would not join such a union if slavery was banned within their borders. Moreover, they were wary of joining a union that might later turn against them. Already, under the Articles of Confederation, which loosely governed the states in the 1780s, one significant change had been enacted. The Northwest Ordinance of 1787 had banned slavery in the newly established Northwest Territory, covering present-day Ohio, Indiana, Illinois, Michigan, Wisconsin, and Minnesota. The Southern states were worried that this ban might spread.

And so their delegates made sure that the wording in the Constitution regarding slavery was very specific.

First, the document guaranteed that the importation of slaves would not be banned for at least twenty years, or until 1808 at the earliest. Second, it allowed for slaves to be counted as three-fifths of a white person for determining a state's population (which mattered particularly for determining how many representatives a state would have in the House of Representatives). So while slaves were legally considered a form of property, for political purposes, they counted for something more.

Opponents of slavery were either disappointed or outraged that the Constitution did not outlaw the practice. But maintaining it was necessary in order to create one united country. As a consolation, slavery opponents were hopeful that the Northwest Ordinance and the prohibition against any further slave importation after 1808 would doom slavery in the long run.

## SLAVERY STUBBORNLY HOLDS ON

As expected, Congress banned the slave trade on the first day legally possible: January 1, 1808. (A year earlier, Great Britain had banned the slave trade throughout its empire.) The ban, however, only referred to the importation of new slaves. Existing slaves were not affected, nor were their children—current or future. All of them could continue to be bought and sold in the United States as their masters wished.

Nevertheless, slavery might well have died out in the South if not for the introduction of a new invention:

The cotton gin removed the seeds from the picked cotton—but slaves still picked cotton by hand up until the invention of the mechanical cotton picker in the 1900s.

the cotton gin. This machine, developed in 1793 by Massachusetts inventor Eli Whitney, efficiently separated cotton fibers from the surrounding seeds. Previously, this painstaking task had been done by hand, which limited cotton's commercial potential. The cotton gin sped up the process and made cotton a more valuable crop than tobacco. Even more fortunate for farmers, the newly settled lands in Alabama and Mississippi were ideal for growing cotton. Cultivating those fields required more labor, which increased the value of African American slaves. Slaves from mid-Atlantic states such as Maryland were increasingly sold to slave owners farther south.

In Congress, slave owners and their representatives continued to protect their interests vigilantly. In 1819, Missouri applied for statehood as a slave state, leading to a new controversy. At that time, there were eleven free states and eleven slave states in the United States as a whole. This balance was no coincidence. Beginning with Vermont and Kentucky in 1791, succeeding states had been admitted to the Union with an eye toward keeping the free and slave states balanced in the Senate (where every state had two members regardless of its population).

The balance did not hold in the House of Representatives, where the more populous Northern states held a majority of 105 to 81 (with the prospect that this gap would only widen over time). Still, representatives of the Northern states worried that bringing Missouri in by itself would give the slave states more influence. Also, Missouri was the first part of the massive Louisiana Purchase to become a state. This territory, bought from France in 1803, stretched from the Mississippi River westward to the Pacific Ocean. If Missouri became a slave state, slavery opponents feared that future states from the region might follow its example.

## THE MISSOURI COMPROMISE

A compromise, spearheaded by Senator Henry Clay of Kentucky, allowed Missouri to enter the Union as a slave state, while Maine entered as a free state. (In the future, it was agreed, slave and free states would continue to be paired.) Also, slavery would now be prohibited in the remaining parts of the Louisiana Purchase north of latitude 36°30' (a line that ran along the bottom of Virginia and Kentucky and just south of the southern borders of present-day Missouri, Kansas, Colorado, and Utah).

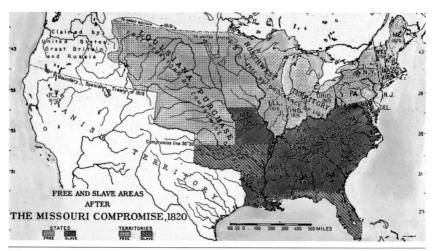

This map of the United States shows the free and slave states and territories created by the Missouri Compromise of 1820.

Despite the Missouri Compromise, pressure increased on Congress to abolish slavery. Laws abolishing slavery had already been passed in many Northern states, but that did not satisfy the abolitionists, as those opposing slavery were called. Fueled by their outrage, the New England Anti-Slavery Society was founded in 1831. A young journalist named William Lloyd Garrison began publishing the most prominent of antislavery newspapers, the *Liberator*, in that same year. Two years later, the American Anti-Slavery Society was created.

As pressure increased on Congress to abolish slavery, some members started petitions to change the existing laws. Proslavery representatives managed to keep such petitions bottled up in committees so they couldn't be debated. In their view, the federal government had no right to interfere with slavery in the states or in the District of Columbia.

# NAT TURNER'S REBELLION

There were hundreds of slave revolts in the United States before the Civil War, but few received much attention. One exception was the 1831 rebellion in Virginia led by the slave Nat Turner. Turner had been taught to read by the son of one of his masters, and he had become known as a forceful preacher. God, he believed, had inspired him to combat slavery by whatever means necessary.

On August 21, Turner, along with six other slaves, began the rebellion by killing his owner and his owner's family. Soon his force grew to about seventy slaves. In all, they killed about sixty whites. After two days, a large force of Virginia militia and volunteers defeated them. Turner himself escaped, but was captured at the end of October. After a quick trial at which he was promptly found guilty, he was hanged on November 11.

Although Turner and his actions served as an inspiration to some, the revolt prompted a crackdown on blacks in the area. Angry whites killed about one hundred innocent slaves. Later, even a hint of resentment on the part of the slaves was met with harsh and swift punishment, making it harder for them to champion their cause.

When the Missouri Compromise was passed, the event probably went unnoticed by one eleven-year-old boy living in Indiana. His name was Abraham Lincoln. He had been born in Kentucky in a log cabin on February 12, 1809. There was nothing remarkable about this at the time. Lots of people were born in log cabins, especially on the frontier. His mother had died when he was nine and his father soon married again. Lincoln and his family eventually moved to Illinois, where Abe became known for his height and his great strength.

Lincoln was largely self-educated. He spent some time as a storekeeper and a surveyor and also served in the Black Hawk War of 1832. He had an unassuming way of relating to people, and he conveyed the impression that he genuinely cared about their welfare. First elected to the Illinois House of Representatives in 1834, he served four terms there. During that time, in 1836, he passed the Illinois bar and officially became a lawyer. The following year, Lincoln publicly expressed his opinion that slavery was "founded both on injustice and bad policy."

Many settlers in Illinois and other western territories disagreed with Lincoln on this point. Certainly, some of them opposed slavery, though even within this group there were many who thought that African Americans were racially inferior. Others might not want slaves themselves, but they didn't particularly care if someone else found them useful.

Amid such contrasting and shaded views, Lincoln was elected to the U.S. House of Representatives in 1846. There he met John Quincy Adams, the former president and current Massachusetts representative. Adams was a staunch abolitionist and had little patience for anyone who thought otherwise. Lincoln also met Senator John C. Calhoun of South Carolina, a man dedicated to preserving slavery in the country for as long as possible.

Calhoun represented the views of many Southern whites. For them, the question of whether slavery was ethical or moral was beside the point. What mattered, they argued, was that slavery was allowed under the Constitution. Therefore any attempt to deny slave owners their rights was unconstitutional. Their slaves were their property, to do with as they wished.

Lincoln spent two years in Washington, just long enough to oppose the Mexican War, which he viewed as a pretext for grabbing land from Mexico, and to support an unsuccessful plan to outlaw slavery in the District of Columbia. He then returned home to Springfield, Illinois, expecting only to resume his position as a successful lawyer.

## THE COUNTRY PULLS APART

Had the number of states remained frozen, perhaps the issue of slavery might have remained manageable (at least from a political standpoint). But the addition of lands to the west, which after the Mexican War included California, made the situation much more volatile.

The Missouri Compromise was thirty years old when another compromise was proposed. Again the issue was balancing the admission of free states and slave states. In this case, it was California that wanted to enter the Union as a free state. The Compromise of 1850 allowed California to do this, but concessions had to be made to proslavery interests: Voters in the newly acquired territories in present-day Utah and New Mexico would be allowed to decide for themselves whether to be free or slave states when the prospect of statehood arose.

At the same time, the Fugitive Slave Act, which Congress had originally passed in 1793, was amended. The avowed purpose of the existing law was to capture escaped slaves and return them to their rightful owners. However, it had proven difficult to enforce and was often ignored in places where antislavery sentiments were strong. The new law was much tougher. Slave owners were given the right to demand the arrest and return of any slave they found up north. And anyone who hid runaways or in any other way hindered the law's enforcement would now face harsh consequences, including a stiff fine and imprisonment.

Despite these risks, a network had grown up to help slaves escape, either to the Northern states or to Canada (where the Fugitive Slave Act had no power to reach them). The people who helped the slaves start on

This painting shows abolitionist leader Harriet Tubman leading escaped slaves to freedom on the "Underground Railroad."

their way were called "agents." The slaves themselves were "passengers" and usually traveled on foot or in wagons. A series of "stations" in private homes (often with secret rooms) were run by "conductors" who helped the escapees.

Thousands of slaves successfully used this "Underground Railroad" to gain their freedom. It was a significant achievement, but their individual triumphs could not overshadow the fact that millions of their fellow slaves were unable to follow their example.

Meanwhile, the tug-of-war between the proslavery and antislavery factions continued. In 1854, Senator Stephen A. Douglas of Illinois proposed a new bill in Congress. Douglas wanted to promote western settlement—settlement that would pass through Chicago, where, not so coincidentally, he owned potentially valuable property. To gain the support of Southerners who had no financial interests of their own in Chicago, Douglas proposed that the existing Nebraska Territory be divided into the Kansas Territory and the Nebraska Territory. Settlers in each place would then decide for themselves whether or not to allow slavery within their borders. Since these territories were both above the 36°30' line that was part of the Missouri Compromise, the change provided a new chance for slavery to spread northward.

The debate over the Kansas-Nebraska Act was bitter, but in the end it passed. One outcome of the debate was the rise of a new political force in the Midwest opposed to slavery. Its name was the Republican Party.

Republicans firmly wished to ban slavery from the territories. So they were not pleased by the verdict in a case that came before the U.S. Supreme Court in 1857. It concerned Dred Scott, a sixty-two-year-old slave who had lived with his master in both the free state of Illinois and the free territory of Wisconsin before they returned to live in the slave state of Missouri. Scott maintained that having lived in places where slavery was prohibited should free him from remaining a slave, even after he moved back to a slave state. The Supreme Court, by a majority of seven to two, ruled that Scott could not bring a suit in a federal court. Chief Justice Roger B. Taney, speaking for the majority, declared that Scott could not do so because blacks were not U.S. citizens. In effect, the ruling stated that

The Supreme Court decision in the *Dred Scott* case was a huge blow to those who wanted to ban slavery from the new U.S. territories—and it paved the way for another decision, which effectively said that slaves were property, not people.

no black person—free or slave—could claim U.S. citizenship, maintaining "that neither the class of persons who had been imported as slaves, nor their descendants, whether they had become free or not" should be given the same rights and protection as white people.

The Court could simply have dismissed the case after ruling on Scott's citizenship. But there was a growing national desire for a ruling on the constitutionality of such laws as the Missouri Compromise. Therefore, the Court discussed this issue as part of its decision in the *Dred Scott* case. It ruled that the Missouri Compromise, which had been repealed in 1854, was unconstitutional. Chief Justice Taney argued that because slaves were property, Congress could not forbid slavery in the territories without violating a slave owner's constitutional right to own property.

This decision was momentous. It effectively erased any advances that African Americans had gained since the days of the Constitution. Slaves were property, not people, and as such they could not take any issues to court.

So, where was the country heading? As it happened, there were two candidates running for the U.S. Senate from Illinois in 1858 who managed to crystallize the issue in a series of seven debates. On one side was the incumbent Democrat Stephen A. Douglas. He was a short man who favored ruffled shirts and jackets with bright buttons. On the other side was Republican Abraham Lincoln, returning to politics after ten years, whose simpler clothes never seemed to properly cover his six-foot-four-inch frame.

Douglas's views supporting slavery were as well known as Lincoln's opposing beliefs. In 1854, Lincoln had made a speech about slavery in which he plainly expressed his opinion:

I hate it because of the monstrous injustice of slavery itself. I hate it because it . . . enables the enemies of free institutions with plausibility to taunt us as hypocrites, causes the real friends of freedom to doubt our sincerity, and especially because it forces so many good men among ourselves into an open war with the very fundamental principles of civil liberty, criticizing the Declaration of Independence, and insisting that there is no right principle of action but self-interest.

The debates between Lincoln and Douglas in 1858 largely centered on the merits and legitimacy of slavery. Neither candidate was an extremist, but their views slanted in opposite directions. In the fifth debate, for example, Lincoln charged that Douglas saw "no end to the institution of slavery." And Douglas did not disagree. "I care more for the great principle of self-government," he replied, "the right of the people to rule, than I do for all the Negroes in Christendom." Months earlier, Lincoln had declared that the delicate balance maintaining slavery in the United States could not last. Having slavery legal in some places but not others was too great a stress for the country to permanently endure.

Lincoln lost the election (at a time when the state legislature, not the general population, actually did the voting), but he had become a figure on the national stage. And once established there, he never left it again.

## A NEW ELECTION AND A NEW WAR

All through the first half of the 1800s, emerging countries in Central and South America had declared themselves free of slavery. The 1850s saw the practice banished in Colombia, Argentina, and Venezuela.

But the United States had not followed their example. And some people were no longer willing to wait for change to come peacefully. In 1859, John Brown, a fiery abolitionist who had been involved in the deaths of five proslavery Southerners in Kansas three years earlier, led an attack on the federal arsenal at Harpers Ferry, Virginia. His aim was to acquire weapons for use in a slave rebellion. The attack was repelled, though, and Brown was captured. He was quickly tried for his crimes and sentenced to death. Even so, Brown never regretted his actions. Before he was hanged, he declared, "I, John Brown, am now quite certain that the crimes of this guilty land will never be purged away but with Blood."

Whether or not Brown was viewed as a martyr, his death stirred strong feelings across the country. And these feelings carried over into the presidential election of 1860. There was no obvious favorite among several candidates. But when the votes were counted, the winner was the Republican Party's Abraham Lincoln, the candidate of the West.

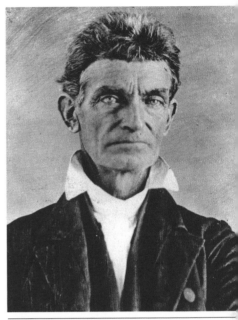

John Brown, an aggressive abolitionist, was so impatient to end slavery that he organized an attack on a federal arsenal so he could steal weapons to arm slaves during a revolt. His attack was unsuccessful, and Brown was hanged for his crimes.

President-elect Lincoln plainly declared that the federal government did not have the authority to eliminate slavery in states where it had always existed. But no matter how many times he said this, Southern leaders refused to trust him. In the face of Lincoln's election, South Carolina senator John C. Calhoun and others were calling for secession.

The Southern states maintained that they had a perfect right to secede from the Union

*"I, John Brown, am now quite certain that the crimes of this guilty land will never be purged away but with Blood."*

*—John Brown, speaking before his death by hanging*

# WILLIAM SEWARD

William H. Seward (1801-1872) was a vocal critic of slavery in the years leading up to the Civil War. Born and raised in New York, he entered politics as a state senator in 1830. His reputation grew rapidly, and he was elected governor in 1838.

Seward was elected a U.S. senator from New York in 1849. He expected to receive the Republican nomination for president in 1860, but instead of campaigning, he left on an extended tour of Europe. Meanwhile, his lesser-known rival, Abraham Lincoln, worked tirelessly to build his own support and eventually received the nomination.

After Lincoln's election, the president-elect asked Seward to serve as secretary of state. On the night of Lincoln's assassination, Seward was wounded at home during an attempt on his own life by an associate of John Wilkes Booth. Seward continued to serve in the cabinet of Lincoln's successor, Andrew Johnson, and in 1867 he oversaw the purchase of Alaska from Russia. At $7,200,000, the purchase promptly earned the name "Seward's folly." Later, however, as the value of Alaska's resources became recognized, Seward's decision was viewed as shrewd and farseeing.

*Above:* William Seward (*seated, at left*), who served in both President Lincoln's cabinet and that of his successor, Andrew Johnson, is shown signing the agreement to purchase Alaska from Russia. Initially called "Seward's folly" because of the large price tag, it was later seen to have been a great deal.

if that action, however drastic, was deemed to be in their best interest. Both Lincoln and the outgoing president, James Buchanan (who would leave office when Lincoln was inaugurated in March 1861), disagreed. Lincoln thought that secession was illegal. The Constitution had included no provision for secession, and without it, he believed, the Southern claim was not defensible.

Sadly, words alone could not settle this argument. Over the winter of 1860–1861, seven states from the South—South Carolina, Mississippi, Florida, Alabama, Georgia, Louisiana, and Texas—seceded from the Union and formed the Confederate States of America. On April 12, 1861, Confederate troops fired on Fort Sumter, the federal fort in the Charleston, South Carolina, harbor. Two days later, the garrison surrendered. By June, four other states—Virginia, Arkansas, North Carolina, and Tennessee—had joined the Confederacy.

And so the Civil War began.

This painting, titled *The Kneeling Slave*, was meant to appeal to the humanity of those who could end the practice of slavery.

AM I NOT A MAN & A BROTHE

# Chapter Two

# A Waiting Game

**ALTHOUGH LINCOLN HAD PUBLICLY** renounced slavery on many occasions before becoming president, he was reluctant to take any immediate action once he reached the White House. His primary concern was to win the war and preserve the Union. He was most concerned about the loyalty of the border states—Delaware, Kentucky, Maryland, Missouri, and West Virginia. (West Virginia was not a state when the war began, but as a region it opposed secession and favored separating from the rest of Virginia. It became a state in 1863.) These states had not followed the Southern states into the Confederacy, but had remained part of the Union. But allegiances there were decidedly mixed. Many slavery supporters lived within their borders. If their position became threatened—if they thought they might lose their slaves—they might well secede and join the Confederacy. So in his first inaugural address,

Lincoln made it plain that he had no intention "directly or indirectly to interfere with the institution of slavery where it exists."

The war went very badly for the North at first. Although the Union side had far greater resources and population than the Confederacy, it was plagued with a series of ineffectual commanders who, either through incompetence or timidity, were unable to make military progress. The Confederate army, headed by the well-respected Robert E. Lee, was not so hobbled. It was also strengthened by the addition of slave labor. The slaves were not allowed to fight for the Confederacy, but they could cook and drive wagons, leaving more white soldiers available for battle. And, of course, the slaves who remained at home minding the fields enabled more Southern farmers to go off and fight.

In the early months of the war, Lincoln continued to follow his policy of restraint regarding abolition. But even as he sought to control the antislavery movement in the greater interests of a Union victory, that movement was sweeping forward on several fronts. Captured slaves, for example, were not being returned to their Confederate owners. The North's reasoning was that the Union army was not returning captured supplies or ammunition, so it should not return slaves either, since by Southern logic, slaves were mere property.

In August 1861, the Union army's Major General John C. Fremont declared martial law in Missouri. As

While Northern commanders floundered during the beginning of the Civil War, the Confederate army, led by General Robert E. Lee, was strengthened by having slaves who could do necessary chores such as cooking and driving the wagons, so that more soldiers were free to fight.

# UNCLE TOM'S CABIN

*Uncle Tom's Cabin* became a national best seller from the moment it was published in 1852, selling more than 300,000 copies in its first year. It told the story of a conflict between Uncle Tom, a long-suffering slave, and his notorious owner, the cruel Simon Legree. The book's author was Harriet Beecher Stowe of Massachusetts (1811–1896), whose family was very much opposed to slavery. The book caused a great outcry, convincing many people that all slave owners were as dastardly as Simon Legree. *Uncle Tom's Cabin* exerted such a great influence that when President Lincoln met Stowe during the Civil War, he reportedly said, "So you're the little woman who wrote the book that made this great war."

Stowe intended Uncle Tom to be perceived as a noble figure fighting adversity. Ironically, the name Uncle Tom later came to refer to any black man who did the bidding of white people with no seeming regard for his own self-respect.

UNCLE TOM'S CABIN

By Harriet Beecher Stowe

**Above:** Harriet Beecher Stowe's novel *Uncle Tom's Cabin* was an enormous best seller. It persuaded many people that slavery was wrong, and it led President Lincoln to give Stowe "credit" for starting the Civil War.

part of this edict, he announced that slaves would be freed from anyone resisting the control of the United States. Lincoln, still trying to balance conflicting loyalties in the region, asked him to revise this order. When Fremont did not, the president had him removed from his post and reassigned elsewhere.

The president could not remove Congress, which passed a law called the Confiscation Act. It stated that when slaves were placed in military service opposing the United States, their owners forfeited all claim to them. Lincoln was reluctant to sign the bill, thinking that it would do little practical good and would only enflame existing passions. Nevertheless, at the urging of several senators, he did sign.

As months passed and the war continued to go badly for the North, Lincoln's position began to shift. He was coming to believe that freeing the slaves might actually be critical to winning the war. In March 1862, Lincoln asked Congress "to pass a joint resolution providing federal aid to any state willing to adopt a plan for the gradual abolition of slavery." However, the border states refused to back the plan. Their objection was that they would be giving up their slaves in return for having remained loyal to the Union. Lincoln tried again in July, but to no avail.

Still, Congress, without the braking influence of the Southern states, was now pursuing a distinctly Northern agenda. In quick succession, Lincoln signed a number

*"Things had gone on from bad to worse until I felt that we had reached the end of our rope . . . ; that we had about played our last card, and must change our tactics, or lose the game!"*

*—Abraham Lincoln, shortly before he issued the Preliminary Emancipation Proclamation*

of bills the legislators put before him. One bill outlawed slavery in the District of Columbia and another banned it from the territories. The bill concerning the capital was notable because it provided owners with compensation that averaged $300 for each slave and included the provision that the freed slaves would be removed to some location outside the district.

Clearly, Lincoln's thinking had changed. By the summer of 1862, he had become convinced that it was necessary to revise his stance on slavery. "Things had gone on from bad to worse," he said, "until I felt that we had reached the end of our rope on the plan of operations we had been pursuing; that we had about played our last card, and must change our tactics, or lose the game!"

The timing, though, was not quite right. Lincoln wanted to wait for a Union military victory, so that his decision to free the slaves in areas under rebellion would not seem to be an act of desperation on the part of a losing army.

So he waited. Some in the government wanted to act quickly, in the belief that the moral imperative out-weighed all others. But Lincoln was a pragmatic man. The proclamation freeing the slaves was a valuable tool. He wanted to make sure it was put to the best possible use. And that meant that morality would have to be put on hold a little while longer.

In 1862, *New York Tribune* editor and abolitionist Horace Greeley criticized President Lincoln for not taking a swifter course of action to end slavery.

# Countdown *to* Freedom

**WAITING HAD ITS AWKWARD MOMENTS.** On August 20, 1862, Horace Greeley, editor of the influential *New York Tribune*, wrote an editorial describing his disappointment with the president's seeming lack of action. Lincoln's supporters, Greeley wrote, were "sorely disappointed and deeply pained by the policy you seem to be pursuing with regard to the slaves of rebels." Lincoln was treating the rebels with far more compassion than they deserved, Greeley believed, and, ironically, with more compassion than he was showing to the millions of people the rebels held under their control. The time for turning back had passed, he wrote. "As one of the millions who would gladly have avoided this struggle at any sacrifice but that of Principle and Honor, but who now feel that the triumph of the Union is indispensable not only to the existence of our country, but to the well-being of mankind, I entreat you to render a hearty and unequivocal obedience to the law of the land."

Greeley was both a prominent editor and an ardent Union supporter, and so Lincoln felt obliged to answer him. On August 25, the *Tribune* published his reply:

> My paramount object in this struggle is to save the Union, and is not either to save or destroy slavery. If I could save the union without freeing any slave I would do it; and if I could save it by freeing all the slaves I would do it; and if I could save it by freeing some and leaving others alone I would also do that. What I do about slavery, and the colored race, I do because I believe it helps to save the Union; and what I forbear, I forbear because I do not believe it would help save the Union.

Lincoln's primary objective was to prosecute the war until victory was won. The proclamation would have to wait until it could do the most good for the Union cause. So he continued to look for the right moment, which finally seemed to come a few weeks later, on September 17. That was when General Lee invaded Maryland, hoping to gain European recognition for the Confederate cause by winning a victory in Union territory. The Battle of Antietam, fought near the town of Sharpsburg, Maryland, was the bloodiest

# FREDERICK DOUGLASS

Frederick Douglass (ca. 1817–1895) was born a slave in Maryland. When he was twelve, his master's wife, Lucretia Auld, taught him the alphabet, even though it was against the law to teach a slave to read. As a young man, he taught other slaves to read, and after escaping to the North, he became a well-known lecturer against slavery. His first autobiography, published in 1845, further cemented his fame. While Douglass was on a lecture tour in England, his supporters purchased his freedom back in Maryland to ensure that he could never be arrested and returned to his former owner.

One of Douglass's favorite sayings was, "I would unite with anybody to do right and with nobody to do wrong." As perhaps the most famous black man in the country, he was among those in the early years of the Civil War who pressed Lincoln to do more to overturn slavery. He maintained that the "Union cause would never prosper till the war assumed an Anti-Slavery attitude, and the Negro was enlisted on the loyal side."

*Above*: This mural by William Edouard Scott illustrates the scene of Frederick Douglass (*right*), freed slave and abolitionist, appealing to President Lincoln and his cabinet to enlist blacks on the Union side.

battle of the Civil War. About 2,000 Northerners and 2,700 Southerners were killed. Nineteen thousand men from both sides were wounded, of whom some 3,000 later died. The Union army, led by General George B. McClellan, did not manage to break through the Confederate lines, however. A last-minute arrival of Southern troops actually saved the day for the Confederacy. However, General Lee's forces suffered such heavy losses that they had to retreat to Virginia. Because Lee retreated, the North called Antietam a Union victory. Five days after the savage battle ended, on September 22, 1862, Lincoln issued the Preliminary Emancipation Proclamation. It stated that if the rebels did not end the fighting and rejoin the Union by January 1, 1863, all slaves in the rebellious states would be free. The Preliminary Proclamation opened with these passages:

> I, Abraham Lincoln, President of the United States of America, and Commander-in-Chief of the Army and Navy thereof, do hereby proclaim and declare that hereafter, as heretofore, the war will be prosecuted for the object of practically restoring the constitutional relation between the United States, and each of the States, and the people thereof, in which States that relation is, or may be, suspended or disturbed.

That it is my purpose, upon the next meeting of Congress to again recommend the adoption of a practical measure tendering pecuniary aid to the free acceptance or rejection of all slave States, so called, the people whereof may not then be in rebellion against the United States and which States may then have voluntarily adopted, or thereafter may voluntarily adopt, immediate or gradual abolishment of slavery within their respective limits; and that the effort to colonize persons of African descent, with their consent, upon this continent, or elsewhere, with the previously obtained consent of the Governments existing there, will be continued.

After the Battle of Antietam was declared a victory for the Union, President Lincoln issued the Preliminary Emancipation Proclamation on September 22, 1862.

That on the first day of January in the year of our Lord, one thousand eight hundred and sixty-three, all persons held as slaves within any State, or designated part of a State, the people whereof shall then be in rebellion against the United States shall be then, thenceforward, and forever free; and the executive government of the United States, including the military and naval authority thereof, will recognize and maintain the freedom of such persons, and will do no act or acts to repress such persons, or any of them, in any efforts they may make for their actual freedom.

The Preliminary Proclamation stated that the current war was being fought to put the Union back together, "restoring the constitutional relation between the United States, and each of the States, and the people thereof, in which States that relation is, or may be, suspended or disturbed."

To meet that goal, Lincoln outlined several possibilities. For states that were part of the Union, compensation would be made for the "immediate or gradual abolishment of slavery within their respective limits." Also, the government would help in any efforts "to colonize persons of African descent, with their consent, upon this continent, or elsewhere."

The mentioning of "consent" here was significant, because Lincoln had for a long time believed that any slaves, once they had obtained their freedom, would be better off being sent to live outside the United States. Lincoln had stated as early as 1854 that his intention "would be to free the slaves and send them back to Liberia, to their own native land." The fact that for many of them their native land was not Liberia, and that they were at least several generations removed from having lived in Africa, did not seem to have troubled him at that time. In August 1862, just a month before issuing the Preliminary Emancipation Proclamation, Lincoln had told a group of freed slaves that "when you cease to be slaves, you are yet far removed from being placed on an equality with the white race." He also told them that Congress had appropriated money in the hope that the former slaves would move somewhere else, perhaps to Central America. He hoped this group would promote such a proposition.

"When you cease to be slaves, you are yet far removed from being placed on an equality with the white race."

—Abraham Lincoln, speaking to a group of freedmen in August 1862

The response to Lincoln's overture was polite within the group itself but less so among the larger black population. As the *Liberator* declared, the nation's slaves "are as much the natives of the country as any of their oppressors. Here they were born; here, by every consideration of justice and humanity, they are entitled to live, and here it is for them to die in the course of nature."

Lincoln's third paragraph established a deadline, January 1, 1863, for implementing the proclamation. On that day, "all persons held as slaves within any State, or designated part of a State, the people whereof shall then be in rebellion against the United States shall be then, thenceforward, and forever free."

# THE PROCLAMATION BECOMES OFFICIAL

One hundred days after the Preliminary Proclamation, with the rebellion unabated, Lincoln issued the Emancipation Proclamation.* The Emancipation Proclamation did not actually free a single slave, because it affected only areas under Confederate control. It excluded slaves in the border states and in Southern areas under Union control, such as Tennessee and parts of Louisiana and Virginia. It was essentially a military measure. Lincoln hoped to inspire all blacks, and especially those enslaved in the Confederacy, to support the Union cause. Most importantly, the freedom it promised depended upon Union military victory.

As the abolitionists had predicted, the Emancipation Proclamation strengthened the North's war effort and weakened the South's. By the end of the war, more than 500,000 slaves had fled to freedom in the North. Since the proclamation announced the acceptance of black men into the Union armed forces, many joined the Union army or navy or worked for them as laborers. By allowing blacks to serve in the military, the Emancipation Proclamation helped solve the North's problem of declining enlistments. About 200,000 black soldiers and sailors, many of them former slaves, served in the armed forces. They helped the North win the war.

*See page 67 for the full text of the Preliminary Emancipation Proclamation and page 71 for the complete text of the Emancipation Proclamation.

The Emancipation Proclamation allowed African Americans to serve in the Union army. One of the approximately 200,000 who did so was Sgt. J. L. Baldwin of Company G, 56th Colored Infantry, which was organized in August 1863.

The Emancipation Proclamation also hurt the South by discouraging Britain and France from entering the war. Both of these nations depended on the South to supply them with cotton, and the Confederacy hoped that they would provide recognition and military aid. But the proclamation made the war a fight against slavery. Most British and French citizens were opposed to slavery and so they gave their support to the North.

While the Emancipation Proclamation did not end slavery in the nation, it did fundamentally transform the character of the war. After January 1, 1863, the war became more and more a war for freedom. Besides strengthening the North militarily and politically, the proclamation added moral force to the Union cause.

In January 1865 Congress ratified the Thirteenth Amendment, which abolished slavery and indentured servitude in the United States. This watercolor shows an African American man reading the headline "Presidential Proclamation, Slavery."

# Chapter Four

# An Ongoing Struggle *for* Justice

**THE CIVIL WAR ENDED ON APRIL 9, 1865.**
In December of that year, the Thirteenth Amendment to the Constitution was ratified. The amendment outlawed slavery throughout the United States, completing the abolition of slavery that the Emancipation Proclamation had begun. The amendment declared that "neither slavery nor involuntary servitude, except as a punishment for crime whereof the party shall have been duly convicted, shall exist within the United States, or any place subject to their jurisdiction."

Making bold changes, however, even legally, did not automatically ensure compliance. There was still considerable resistance in some states to accepting former slaves as equals under the law. And so three years later, the Fourteenth Amendment was passed to clear up any confusion or willful disregard for the existing law.

Section 1 stated that:

all persons born or naturalized in the United States, and subject to the jurisdiction thereof, are citizens of the United States and of the State wherein they reside. No State shall make or enforce any law which shall abridge the privileges or immunities of citizens of the United States; nor shall any State deprive any person of life, liberty, or property, without due process of law; nor deny to any person within its jurisdiction the equal protection of the laws.

That could have settled the matter—except that it didn't. African Americans might be technically free, but their status as equal citizens under the law was still being resisted. One distinctive right, the right to vote, drew particular attention, as former proponents of slavery designed new restrictions to keep blacks from voting. To combat this trend, the Fifteenth Amendment was added in 1870. It was a short amendment, plainly stating, "The right of citizens of the United States to vote shall not be denied or abridged by the United States or by any State on account of race, color, or previous condition of servitude."

The Fifteenth Amendment was the third attempt to create a legal foundation for the Emancipation Proclamation, one that in principle would be obeyed and enforced throughout the country. Unfortunately, like the

Thirteenth and Fourteenth Amendments, it failed to do so. Southern states in particular remained unwilling to grant African Americans the same rights that white citizens enjoyed. And the country as a whole, still licking its wounds from the recent bloodshed, was reluctant to offer much more than the amendments themselves.

## RECOVERY AND RECONSTRUCTION

In the period immediately following the Civil War, Northern officials took control of the former Confederate states. There were many issues to address. The South faced enormous problems in rebuilding itself. Cities such as Atlanta, Georgia, and Richmond, Virginia, lay in ruins. Railway lines were destroyed. Thousands of newly freed slaves needed help in beginning new lives.

Reconstruction, as this period was called, lasted from 1865 to 1877. During this time, along with the passage of the Thirteenth, Fourteenth, and Fifteenth Amendments, small advances were made for African Americans. Laws were passed to protect their rights; schools were set up to provide them with education. After twelve years and considerable resistance on the part of the Southern states, however, the North pretty much lost interest in Reconstruction. Southerners regained control of their state governments and quickly did away with many of the rights that blacks had won. They were determined that African Americans, however free, should not be integrated into white society.

Maybe the new constitutional amendments could not be directly opposed but, with a little imagination, they could be circumvented. Wherever possible, the politicians created new legal barriers to equality. And in circumstances where this was not feasible, they relied on fear and intimidation to keep blacks in their place.

Even after the passage of the Fifteenth Amendment, voting remained a crucial issue. Why? White Southerners feared that African Americans would use their numbers to collectively institute political reforms. Such reforms would upset the balance of power in the white establishment. The best way to keep this from happening was simply to prevent blacks from voting at all. Different political and legal strategies were employed for this purpose. In some Southern states, people could vote only if their grandfathers had voted before Reconstruction. Other states required voters to pass literacy tests. (Many former slaves had never been allowed to learn to read.) Some states instituted a head tax, or poll tax, whereby all citizens would have to pay a fee in order to register to vote in an election. Few African Americans had the means to pay such a tax.

Voting restrictions were just the beginning. In one situation after another, white people and white-owned businesses practiced racial discrimination pretty much as they pleased. Some disputes ended up in court, sometimes with appeals to the highest level. But time and again, the U.S. Supreme Court sided with the local governments.

Most significantly, the 1896 case *Plessy v. Ferguson*

upheld a Louisiana law that created "separate but equal" areas on its railroad cars. The case began in 1892, when an African American shoemaker named Homer A. Plessy challenged a Louisiana law that required separate but equal facilities for blacks and whites in railroad cars. John H. Ferguson, a district court judge, rejected Plessy's plea that the law was unconstitutional. The case eventually reached the Supreme Court. Plessy's lawyers argued that the law violated a clause of the Fourteenth Amendment that guaranteed American citizens equal protection under the laws. The Court upheld the Louisiana law, ruling that the amendment did not seek to guarantee the social equality of all the races. Once this legal precedent was established, other restrictions quickly sprang up across the South, segregating everything from hotels to restaurants to drinking fountains. The Jim Crow era had come into full swing, and it would last a very long time.

The Jim Crow era ushered in segregated hotels, restaurants, waiting rooms for transportation, and even drinking fountains. Though based on a law allowing "separate but equal" facilities, the separation was anything *but* equal.

The gradual push to fulfill the spirit of the Emancipation Proclamation became stronger in the middle of the twentieth century. Previously, black leaders such as Booker T. Washington, a former slave who had founded a school in Tuskegee, Alabama, believed in making gradual improvements from within the system. Other figures, though, believed that true progress could only come through more dramatic means.

For many years, African Americans worked to end segregation on various fronts. The U.S. armed forces were finally integrated in 1948, thanks to an executive order issued by President Harry Truman. Sports saw its first desegregation with the addition of baseball great Jackie Robinson to the Brooklyn Dodgers in 1947. Other changes reflected progress in areas that had been under pressure for decades, particularly public education. The National Association for the Advancement of Colored People (NAACP) had long been fighting against inequality in education. The breakthrough came in the 1954 Supreme Court case of *Brown v. Board of Education*. Here the Court overturned the long-standing rule of "separate but equal," when Thurgood Marshall, the NAACP's attorney, successfully argued that separate educational facilities could never be equal. The Court thus declared racial segregation in public schools to be unconstitutional, and schools were ordered to desegregate "with all deliberate speed." That phrase

# THURGOOD MARSHALL

Thurgood Marshall (1908–1993) was the first African American to become a U.S. Supreme Court justice. The great-grandson of slaves, he was born and raised in Baltimore, Maryland. His original first name was Thoroughgood, but he shortened it to Thurgood in the second grade. After graduating from college, he had hoped to attend the University of Maryland School of Law, but was told that he would not be admitted because of his color. Instead, he attended law school at Howard University, graduating in 1933.

Five years later, Marshall became chief counsel for the NAACP. He had many successes in civil rights cases, leading up to his victory in the landmark case of *Brown v. Board of Education* in 1954. He was appointed to the U.S. Court of Appeals in 1961 and then to the Supreme Court in 1967. He served for twenty-four years before retiring in 1991.

*Above:* After graduating from college, Thurgood Marshall applied to the University of Maryland School of Law but was denied admission because of his race. After receiving his law degree from Howard University, a noted black institution, Marshall devoted his life to fighting for racial equality.

was perhaps unfortunate, as it led many communities to focus on the "deliberate" at the expense of the "speed."

By this time, the frustrations and impatience with the existing system were beginning to pile up. The next year, in Montgomery, Alabama, an NAACP secretary named Rosa Parks refused to give up her seat on the bus to a white passenger. Parks later explained: "People always say that I didn't give up my seat because I was tired, but that isn't true. I was not tired physically, or no more tired than I usually was at the end of a working day. I was not old, although some people have an image of me as being old then. I was forty-two. No, the only tired I was, was tired of giving in."

Parks was arrested for not giving up her seat. That sparked a boycott of the bus company. The boycott was led by a twenty-six-year-old minister named Dr. Martin Luther King Jr. Other nonviolent protests and similar forms of civil disobedience followed, including the 1960 Greensboro sit-in (protesting segregated lunch counters in North Carolina) and the March on Washington in August 1963. It was at that gathering that Dr. King looked out over a throng of 200,000 people in front of the Lincoln Memorial and gave his famous "I have a dream" speech, which focused on the hope that racial discrimination would one day end once and for all.

Unfortunately, there were also times when violence erupted. On March 7, 1965, police attacked six

After almost one hundred years of continued postslavery racial segregation in the South, Dr. Martin Luther King Jr. led the March on Washington and gave his famous "I have a dream" speech, witnessed by a crowd of 200,000 people, in front of the Lincoln Memorial.

# THE NAACP

The NAACP was founded on February 12, 1909, on the hundredth anniversary of Lincoln's birthday. Its leaders were determined to fight all forms of segregation "to ensure the political, educational, social, and economic equality of rights of all persons and to eliminate racial hatred and racial discrimination." The NAACP realized that a key component of black advancement was education, and one of its most important goals was to improve educational opportunities for African American children.

In its early years, the NAACP had some success raising awareness about racial injustice. It also registered some concrete victories; for example, getting black officers into the army in World War I and fighting lynching in the South in the 1930s. The organization was very active during the civil rights movement of the 1960s and continues to advocate for equal treatment for American blacks today.

*Above*: The NAACP was founded in 1909, the hundredth anniversary of President Lincoln's birthday, to fight racial segregation, and it continues to do so to this day.

hundred civil rights activists attempting to march the fifty-four miles from Selma to Montgomery, Alabama. Two days later, another march was stopped as well. On a third attempt, the demonstrators completed the route. The marches were meant to draw attention to the inequities forced on black voters in Alabama. Although 50 percent of Alabama's population was African American, blacks made up only one percent of registered voters.

Real progress was made in federal elections following the ratification of the Twenty-fourth Amendment to the Constitution. This amendment declared that citizens could not be denied their right to vote in federal elections for failing to pay "any poll tax or other tax."

Finally, the comprehensive Civil Rights Act of 1964 brought at least a legal end to the discrimination that had festered since Reconstruction. This act made discrimination illegal in all hotels, restaurants, theaters, and other public places. It also prohibited state and local governments from imposing restrictions that would deny access to public facilities on the basis of race, religion, gender, or ethnicity. It encouraged desegregation of schools and prohibited discrimination in any activity that received federal funding.

Still, the anger that had simmered for a century could not be easily cooled. The summer of 1968 was a period of great unrest following the assassination in

April of Dr. King. In the 1970s, court-ordered busing, which was meant to ensure that public schools were integrated even if their local neighborhoods were not, sparked a number of protests.

However, there were advances to report as well. In 1940, only 5 percent of voting-age Southern blacks were registered. By 1972, the figure approached 60 percent and was still rising. As more and more blacks began to vote, an increasing number of black candidates were elected. The last barrier to political progress was breached with the 2008 election of Barack Obama as the nation's first black president.

# Conclusion

**IN NOVEMBER 1942, DURING THE MIDDLE** of World War II, British prime minister Winston Churchill, speaking of recent victories in North Africa, famously stated, "Now this is not the end. It is not even the beginning of the end. But it is, perhaps, the end of the beginning."

So too the Emancipation Proclamation was not a final reckoning, but simply the end of the beginning of slavery in America. A process that began the day Columbus first set foot in the New World had grown into an ethical and moral monstrosity by the end of the eighteenth century. It remained a festering weakness in the U.S. Constitution, a document that purported to usher in a new democratic era, and the continued acceptance of slavery created a vulnerability that plagued the first seventy years of the new nation.

The Civil War was meant to change all that. And it did usher in the proclamation itself, which many people felt was long overdue. Even so, the proclamation was a wartime announcement, part practical measure and part symbolic gesture. Certainly, it represented a significant step in the right direction. It did not, though, put things to rights once and for all.

It did, however, trigger a chain of events, amendments, and new laws that finally eradicated the vestiges of slavery from the American legal system. And that certainly represented progress, though it took more than a hundred years to accomplish. Still, it would be unwise for Americans to sit back and imagine that the work of eliminating racial prejudice is all but finished. Like a little demon in the back of one's brain, bigotry can strike out when least expected. Nevertheless, a country in which a black president was elected less than fifty years after the Civil Rights Act outlawed racial discrimination and segregation can legitimately hope that the future looks far brighter than the past.

# The Preliminary Emancipation Proclamation

## September 22, 1862

FROM THE U.S. NATIONAL ARCHIVES & RECORDS ADMINISTRATION

---

## By the President of the United States of America.

## A Proclamation.

I, Abraham Lincoln, President of the United States of America, and Commander-in-Chief of the Army and Navy thereof, do hereby proclaim and declare that hereafter, as heretofore, the war will be prosecuted for the object of practically restoring the constitutional relation between the United States, and each of the States, and the people thereof, in which States that relation is, or may be, suspended or disturbed.

That it is my purpose, upon the next meeting of Congress to again recommend the adoption of a practical measure tendering pecuniary aid to the free acceptance or rejection of all slave States, so called, the people whereof may not then be in rebellion against the United States and which States may then have voluntarily adopted, or thereafter may voluntarily adopt, immediate or gradual abolishment of slavery within their respective limits; and that the effort to colonize persons of African descent, with their consent, upon this continent, or elsewhere, with the previously obtained consent of the Governments existing there, will be continued.

That on the first day of January in the year of our Lord, one thousand eight hundred and sixty-three, all persons held as slaves within any State, or designated part of a State, the people whereof shall then be in rebellion against the United States shall be then, thenceforward, and forever free; and the executive government of the United States, including the military and naval authority thereof, will recognize and maintain the freedom of such persons, and will do no act or acts to repress such persons, or any of them, in any efforts they may make for their actual freedom.

That the executive will, on the first day of January aforesaid, by proclamation, designate the States, and part of States, if any, in which the people thereof respectively, shall then be in rebellion against the United States; and the fact that any State, or the people thereof shall, on that day be, in good faith represented in the Congress of the United States, by members chosen thereto, at elections wherein a majority of the qualified voters of such State shall have participated, shall, in the absence of strong countervailing testimony, be deemed conclusive evidence that such State and the people thereof, are not then in rebellion against the United States.

That attention is hereby called to an Act of Congress entitled "An Act to make an additional Article of War" approved March 13, 1862, and which act is in the words and figure following:

"Be it enacted by the Senate and House of Representatives of the United States of America in Congress assembled, That hereafter the following shall be promulgated as an additional article of war for the government of the army of the United States, and shall be obeyed and observed as such:

"Article–All officers or persons in the military or naval service of the United States are prohibited from employing any of the forces under their respective commands for the purpose of returning fugitives from service or labor, who may have escaped from any persons to whom such service or labor is claimed to be due, and any officer who shall be found guilty by a court martial of violating this article shall be dismissed from the service.

"Sec. 2. And be it further enacted, That this act shall take effect from and after its passage."

Also to the ninth and tenth sections of an act entitled "An Act to suppress Insurrection, to punish Treason and Rebellion, to seize and confiscate property of rebels, and for other purposes," approved July 17, 1862, and which sections are in the words and figures following:

"Sec. 9. And be it further enacted, That all slaves of persons who shall hereafter be engaged in rebellion against the government of the United States, or who shall in any way give aid or comfort thereto, escaping from such persons and taking refuge within the lines of the army; and all slaves captured from such persons or deserted by them and coming under the control of the government of the United States; and all slaves of such persons found on (or) being within any place occupied by rebel forces and afterwards occupied by the forces of the United States, shall be deemed captives of war, and shall be forever free of their servitude and not again held as slaves.

"Sec. 10. And be it further enacted, That no slave escaping into any State, Territory, or the District of Columbia, from any other State, shall be delivered up, or in any way impeded or hindered of his liberty, except for crime, or some offence against the laws, unless the person claiming said fugitive shall first make oath that the person to whom the labor or service of such fugitive is alleged to be due is his lawful owner, and has not borne arms against the United States in the present rebellion, nor in any way given aid and comfort thereto; and no person engaged in the military or naval service of the United States shall, under any pretence whatever, assume to decide on the validity of the claim of any person to the service or labor of any other person, or surrender up any such person to the claimant, on pain of being dismissed from the service."

And I do hereby enjoin upon and order all persons engaged in the military and naval service of the United States to observe, obey, and enforce, within their respective spheres of service, the act, and sections above recited.

And the executive will in due time recommend that all citizens of the United States who shall have remained loyal thereto throughout the rebellion, shall (upon the restoration of the constitutional relation between the United States, and their respective States, and people, if that relation shall have been suspended or disturbed) be compensated for all losses by acts of the United States, including the loss of slaves.

In witness whereof, I have hereunto set my hand, and caused the seal of the United States to be affixed.

Done at the City of Washington this twenty-second day of September, in the year of our Lord, one thousand, eight hundred and sixty-two, and of the Independence of the United States the eighty seventh.

By the President: *Abraham Lincoln*

*William H. Seward, Secretary of State*

# The Emancipation Proclamation
## January 1, 1863

FROM THE U.S. NATIONAL ARCHIVES &
RECORDS ADMINISTRATION

---

## By the President of the United States of America.

## A Proclamation.

Whereas, on the twenty-second day of September, in the year of our Lord one thousand eight hundred and sixty-two, a proclamation was issued by the President of the United States, containing, among other things, the following, to wit:

"That on the first day of January, in the year of our Lord one thousand eight hundred and sixty-three, all persons held as slaves within any State or designated part of a State, the people whereof shall then be in rebellion against the United States, shall be then, thenceforward, and forever free; and the Executive Government of the United States, including the military and naval authority thereof, will recognize and maintain the freedom of such persons, and will do no act or acts to repress such persons, or any of them, in any efforts they may make for their actual freedom.

"That the Executive will, on the first day of January aforesaid, by proclamation, designate the States and parts of States, if any, in which the people thereof, respectively, shall then be in rebellion against the United States; and the fact that any State, or the people thereof, shall on that day be, in good faith, represented in the Congress of the United States by members chosen thereto at elections wherein a majority of the qualified voters of such State shall have participated, shall, in the absence of strong countervailing testimony, be deemed conclusive evidence that such State, and the people thereof, are not then in rebellion against the United States."

Now, therefore I, Abraham Lincoln, President of the United States, by virtue of the power in me vested as Commander-in-Chief, of the Army and Navy of the United States in time of actual armed rebellion against the authority and government of the United States, and as a fit and necessary war measure for suppressing said rebellion, do, on this first day of January, in the year of our Lord one thousand eight hundred and sixty-three, and in accordance with my purpose so to do publicly proclaimed for the full period of one hundred days, from the day first above mentioned, order and designate as the States and parts of States wherein the people thereof respectively, are this day in rebellion against the United States, the following, to wit:

Arkansas, Texas, Louisiana, (except the Parishes of St. Bernard, Plaquemines, Jefferson, St. John, St. Charles, St. James Ascension, Assumption, Terrebonne, Lafourche, St. Mary, St. Martin, and Orleans, including the City of New Orleans) Mississippi, Alabama, Florida, Georgia, South Carolina, North Carolina, and Virginia, (except the forty-eight counties designated as West Virginia, and also the counties of Berkley, Accomac, Northampton, Elizabeth City, York, Princess Ann, and Norfolk, including the cities of Norfolk and Portsmouth[)], and which excepted parts, are for the present, left precisely as if this proclamation were not issued.

And by virtue of the power, and for the purpose aforesaid, I do order and declare that all persons held as slaves within said designated States, and parts of States, are, and henceforward shall be free; and that the Executive government of the United States, including the military and naval authorities thereof, will recognize and maintain the freedom of said persons.

And I hereby enjoin upon the people so declared to be free to abstain from all violence, unless in necessary self-defence; and I recommend to them that, in all cases when allowed, they labor faithfully for reasonable wages.

And I further declare and make known, that such persons of suitable condition, will be received into the armed service of the United States to garrison forts, positions, stations, and other places, and to man vessels of all sorts in said service.

And upon this act, sincerely believed to be an act of justice, warranted by the Constitution, upon military necessity, I invoke the considerate judgment of mankind, and the gracious favor of Almighty God.

In witness whereof, I have hereunto set my hand and caused the seal of the United States to be affixed.

Done at the City of Washington, this first day of January, in the year of our Lord one thousand eight hundred and sixty three, and of the Independence of the United States of America the eighty-seventh.

*By the President: Abraham Lincoln*

*William H. Seward, Secretary of State*

# NOTES

## A Sign of Things to Come

p. 7, "A house divided . . .": David Herbert Donald, *Lincoln* (New York: Simon and Schuster, 1995), 206.

## Chapter One: Slavery in America

p. 15, "waged cruel war . . .": Carl Becker, *The Declaration of Independence* (New York: Random House, 1970), 147.

p. 22, "founded both on injustice . . .": John Hope Franklin, *The Emancipation Proclamation* (Garden City, NY: Doubleday, 1963), 21.

p. 28, "that neither the class . . .": Henry Steele Commager, ed., *Documents of American History*, 9th ed. (Englewood Cliffs, NJ: Prentice-Hall, 1973), 1: 341.

p. 29, "I hate it . . .": Peter Burchard, *Lincoln and Slavery* (New York: Atheneum, 1999), 43.

p. 29, "no end to . . .": Mark C. Carnes, ed., *U.S. History, Macmillan Information Now Encyclopedia* (New York: Macmillan, 1998), 363.

p. 29, "I care more . . .": Ibid.

p. 30, "I, John Brown . . .": Ibid., 35.

## Chapter Two: A Waiting Game

p. 36, "directly or indirectly . . .": Henry Steele Commager, ed., *Documents of American History*, 9th ed. (Englewood Cliffs, NJ: Prentice-Hall, 1973), 1:385.

p. 38, "So you're the . . .": Fred R. Shapiro, ed., *The Yale Book of Quotations* (New Haven, CT: Yale University Press, 2006), 465.

p. 39, "to pass a . . .": Doris Kearns Goodwin, *Team of Rivals: The Political Genius of Abraham Lincoln* (New York: Simon and Schuster, 2005), 459.

p. 40, "Things had gone . . .": John Hope Franklin, *The*

*Emancipation Proclamation* (Garden City, NY: Doubleday, 1963), 35.

CHAPTER THREE: COUNTDOWN TO FREEDOM

p. 43, "sorely disappointed . . .": John Hope Franklin, *The Emancipation Proclamation* (Garden City, NY: Doubleday, 1963), 27.

p. 43, "As one of the . . .": Ibid.

p. 44, "My paramount object . . .": Ibid., 28.

p. 45, "I would unite . . .": Frederick Douglass, *The Anti Slavery Movement, A Lecture* (Rochester, NY: Lee, Mann and Co., 1855), 33.

p. 45, "Union cause . . .": John Hope Franklin, *The Emancipation Proclamation* (Garden City, NY: Doubleday, 1963), 25.

p. 46, "I, Abraham Lincoln . . .": Ibid., 50.

p. 48, "would be to free . . .": Ibid., 33.

p. 49, "when you cease . . .": Doris Kearns Goodwin, *Team of Rivals: The Political Genius of Abraham Lincoln* (New York: Simon and Schuster, 2005), 469.

p. 49, "are as much . . .": Ibid.

CHAPTER FOUR: AN ONGOING STRUGGLE FOR JUSTICE

p. 53, "neither slavery . . .": Henry Steele Commager, ed., *Documents of American History*, 9th ed. (Englewood Cliffs, NJ: Prentice-Hall, 1973), 2:813.

p. 54, "all persons born . . .": Ibid.

p. 54, "The right of . . .": Ibid., 2: 814.

p. 60, "People always say. . .": Rosa Parks, *Rosa Parks: My Story* (New York: Dial Books, 1992), 116.

p. 62, "to ensure the . . .": *NAACP*, at http://www.naacp.org/about/mission/

p. 63, "any poll tax . . .": Henry Steele Commager, ed., *Documents of American History*, 9th ed. (Englewood Cliffs, NJ: Prentice-Hall, 1973), 2:816.

CONCLUSION

p. 65, "Now this is . . .": John Bartlett, *Bartlett's Familiar Quotations*, 16th ed., edited by Justin Kaplan (Boston: Little, Brown and Company, 1992), 621.

## FOR FURTHER INFORMATION

BOOKS

Blight, David W. *A Slave No More*. New York: Harcourt, 2007.

Goodwin, Doris Kearns. *Team of Rivals: The Political Genius of Abraham Lincoln*. New York: Simon and Schuster, 2005.

Meltzer, Milton. *A. Lincoln in His Own Words*. New York: Harcourt, Brace and Company, 1993.

Schneider, Dorothy, and Carl Schneider. *Slavery in America: From Colonial Times to the Civil War*. New York: Facts on File, 2000.


WEBSITES

Abraham Lincoln Papers: Emancipation Proclamation
http://memory.loc.gov/ammem/alhtml/almintr.html
    This Library of Congress site provides background and a time line tracing the events surrounding the development of the proclamation.

The Emancipation Proclamation
www.archives.gov/exhibits/featured_documents/
emancipation_proclamation
    The U.S. Government Archives feature a close-up look at the Emancipation Proclamation, including Lincoln's own handwritten text and a description of the surrounding events.

Lincoln's Greatest Quotes
www.theamericans.us/Quote.html
    This sampling of Abraham Lincoln quotations features his wit, wisdom, and approach to writing.

# SELECTED BIBLIOGRAPHY

Burchard, Peter. *Lincoln and Slavery*. New York: Atheneum, 1999.

Carnes, Mark C., ed. *U.S. History. Macmillan Information Now Encyclopedia*. New York: Simon and Schuster, 1998.

Donald, David Herbert. *Lincoln*. New York: Macmillan, 1995.

Franklin, John Hope. *The Emancipation Proclamation*. Garden City, NY: Doubleday, 1963.

Goodwin, Doris Kearns. *Team of Rivals: The Political Genius of Abraham Lincoln*. New York: Simon and Schuster, 2005.

Guelzo, Allen C. *Lincoln's Emancipation Proclamation: The End of Slavery in America*. New York: Simon and Schuster, 2004.

Ketcham, Henry. *The Life of Abraham Lincoln*. Middlesex, England: Echo Library, 2008.

# INDEX

## ABOUT THE AUTHOR

STEPHEN KRENSKY is the author of more than one hundred fiction and nonfiction books for children, including many about American history. He has written chapter-book biographies of Barack Obama, Benjamin Franklin, and George Washington as well as shorter works on the Salem witch trials, Paul Revere, John Adams, the California gold rush, George Washington Carver, Annie Oakley, and the Wright Brothers.